**W9-AXU-723**

8/00

DOCTORS IN ACTION

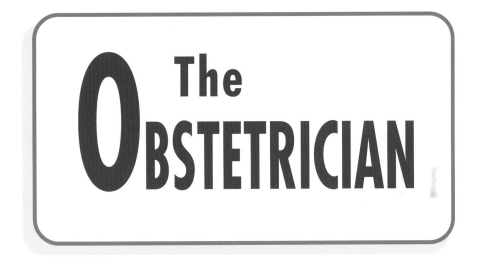

The OBSTETRICIAN

by
Lee Jacobs

Photographs by
Gale Zucker

BLACKBIRCH PRESS, INC.
WOODBRIDGE, CONNECTICUT

Published by Blackbirch Press, Inc.
260 Amity Road
Woodbridge, CT 06525

©1999 by Blackbirch Press, Inc.
First Edition

e-mail: staff@blackbirch.com
Web site: www.blackbirch.com

Printed in the United States

10 9 8 7 6 5 4 3 2 1

Acknowledgments
The publisher would like to thank Fletcher Allen Health Care and Yale-New Haven Hospital for their valuable cooperation in putting this project together.

Page 9: Artwork by Sonja Kalter

For Jacob, Sarah
and Leah
L.J.

Library of Congress Cataloging-in-Publication Data
Jacobs, Lee.
Obstetrician/ by Lee Jacobs.
     p.   cm. — (Doctors in action.)
   Includes bibliographical references and index.
   Summary: Follows the activities of Dr. Ellie Wegner, an obstetrician and gynecologist, introducing facts about what these doctors do and the specialized training they get, as well as providing information about human reproduction and gestation.
   ISBN 1-56711-235-8 (lib. bdg. : alk. paper)
   1. Obstetricians—Juvenile literature. 2. Obstetrics—Juvenile literature.
[1. Obstetrician. 2. Obstetrics. 3. Occupations.] I. Title. II. Series.
RG525.5.J3   1999   98-9877
618.2—dc21   CIP
                                                                                                        AC

hances are good that, when your mother was pregnant with you, she visited an obstetrician (ob•ste•tri•shen). An obstetrician is a doctor that specializes in pregnancy and birth.

While she is pregnant, a woman goes to her obstetrician each month. The doctor talks to the mother about eating well and getting enough exercise. An obstetrician will also tell patients about things that are unhealthy for babies, such as smoking and drinking. At each visit, the obstetrician carefully keeps track of the baby's growth.

After about 9 months, the patient is ready to give birth to (deliver) her baby. The obstetrician is there to help in the delivery. Giving birth is hard work. It can take many hours. Usually an obstetrician and a team of nurses and midwives (nurses that are specially trained in obstetrics) will monitor the progress of both the mother and the baby during the labor (pre-birth) period. Once the baby is born, the obstetrician continues to care for the mother for several weeks.

Obstetricians and midwives are also trained in another kind of medicine called gynecology (gy•ne•kology). Gynecologists deal with women's reproductive organs.

Because obstetrics and gynecology are practiced together, an obstetrician/gynecologist often becomes a woman's main doctor. This doctor-patient relationship can last from the time a woman is in her teens until she is in her sixties or seventies.

Giving birth is often long, hard work. Afterwards, rest is needed to regain strength.

Dr. Ellie Wegner has been an obstetrician/gynecologist for more than 7 years. She decided that she wanted to become an obstetrician because she thought it would be wonderful to take care of moms and new babies. She also wanted to share in such a happy part of people's lives.

Dr. Wegner's day begins very early in the morning and ends in the evening. She starts out by doing "rounds" at the local hospital. "Rounding" means visiting patients in the hospital.

Dr. Wegner's patients may be in the hospital for a few different reasons. Some are brand new mothers. Dr. Wegner visits with them to see how they are feeling and to answer questions. (A pediatrician, a doctor who specializes in caring for children, will usually visit to check on the newborn.) Dr. Wegner also has patients whose babies were delivered a special way called "c-section," or cesarean section. This is a kind of surgery. An obstetrician makes a cut in the mother's abdomen and uterus to take the baby out.

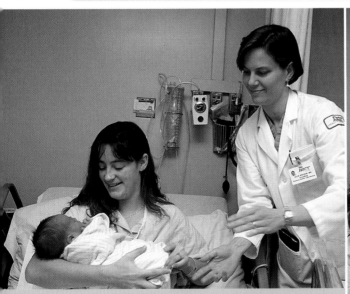

Above: *Dr. Wegner checks on a new mom and her newborn.*
Right: *A pediatrician is usually on hand to examine the newborn.*

HOW AN UNBORN BABY DEVELOPS

The period of time in which an unborn baby develops is called gestation (jess•tay•shun). This is the time from fertilization of an egg to a baby's birth. In humans, gestation generally lasts 280 days, or about 9 months. A fertilized egg is made up of one cell. But this cell quickly begins to divide and then multiply. It divides and multiplies over and over again until there are billions of cells.

During gestation, a baby goes through many stages of development. For the first 8 weeks, the developing human is called an embryo. After the eighth week, it is called a fetus. The 9 months of pregnancy are often broken down into 3 time periods called trimesters. Each trimester is about 3 months long.

First Trimester

By the end of the first trimester, the fetus weighs about 1 ounce and is about 4 inches long. The nerves that form the brain begin to develop during this time. And a face and four limbs have formed—complete with fingers and toes!

Second Trimester

In the second trimester, hair, eyebrows, and eyelashes start to grow. By the end of the second trimester, the fetus weighs about 1 pound and the bones of its skeleton are developing quickly. This tiny baby can already open and close its eyes, suck its thumb, and kick!

Third Trimester

By the end of the eighth month, the baby weighs about 5 pounds and is about 18 inches long. The brain is still growing rapidly, and the baby can both see and hear. Most of the baby's systems are developed by this time. In the last month, the baby grows a lot—it usually gets a few inches longer and adds a few pounds! Its lungs are now mature and it is ready to be born.

The Three Stages of Pregnancy

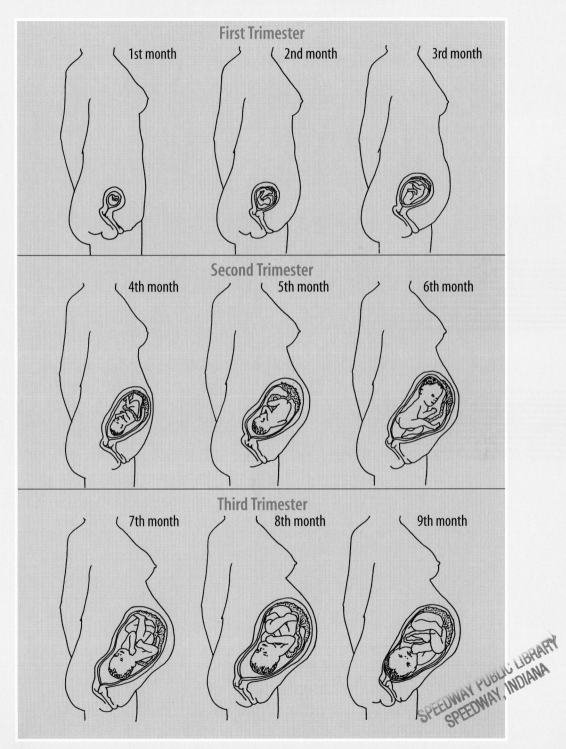

First Trimester — 1st month, 2nd month, 3rd month

Second Trimester — 4th month, 5th month, 6th month

Third Trimester — 7th month, 8th month, 9th month

3131

After Dr. Wegner finishes checking on her patients at the hospital, she goes to her office. In the office, Dr. Wegner, the nurses, and midwives examine patients. They check weight and blood pressure. They want to see that the mom is gaining enough weight for the healthy growth of the baby.

To check blood pressure, a soft band is strapped around the patient's arm. Then the band is pumped up with air. As the air is released, a stethoscope and a gauge on the armband are used to read the blood pressure.

After several weeks, a special kind of "machine" is used to amplify sounds from inside the pregnant woman. It allows everyone to listen to the baby's heartbeat!

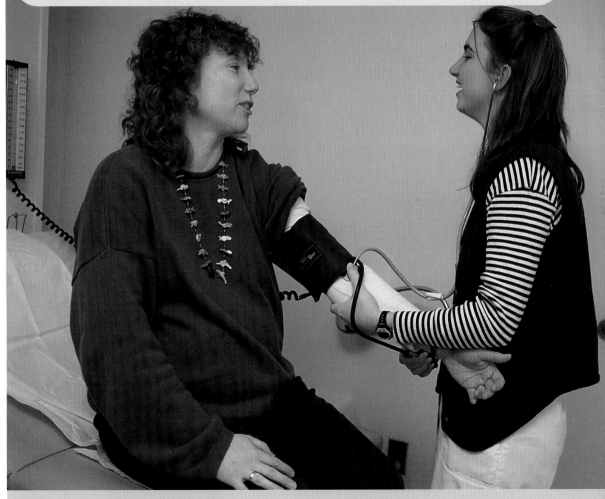

Blood pressure is checked regularly.

Many women check on the developing fetus in another way. This is done with a process called ultrasound. An ultrasound machine actually lets you see a baby inside a woman's body! The machine uses high-frequency sound waves to form a picture of a baby on a television-type monitor.

An ultrasound is painless. A pregnant woman lays down and a wand is passed over her belly. The wand sends sound waves through the skin. The picture that is created is shown on the screen. Ultrasounds can show many things about a baby. It allows a doctor to check that all of the baby's organs are developing normally. It offers a view of arms and legs, and is a good way to measure the baby. This is also how some people see if they are going to have a boy or girl!

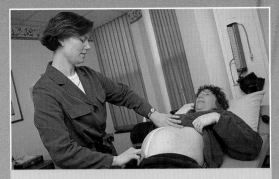

Above: *Belly measurements help with tracking the baby's growth.*

An ultrasound machine provides doctors and patients with important information.

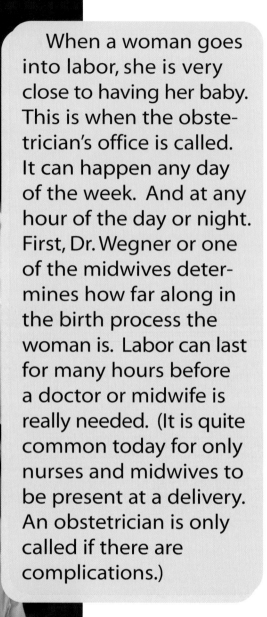

When a woman goes into labor, she is very close to having her baby. This is when the obstetrician's office is called. It can happen any day of the week. And at any hour of the day or night. First, Dr. Wegner or one of the midwives determines how far along in the birth process the woman is. Labor can last for many hours before a doctor or midwife is really needed. (It is quite common today for only nurses and midwives to be present at a delivery. An obstetrician is only called if there are complications.)

Dr. Wegner gets a message on her beeper.

There are many other health care workers who help both the mom and the obstetrician during the birth process. Some of these people are the mid-wives. Others are called labor and delivery nurses. They are specially trained in assisting women through labor. Another important helper can be an anesthe-siologist, who provides special medication to ease the pain during labor and delivery.

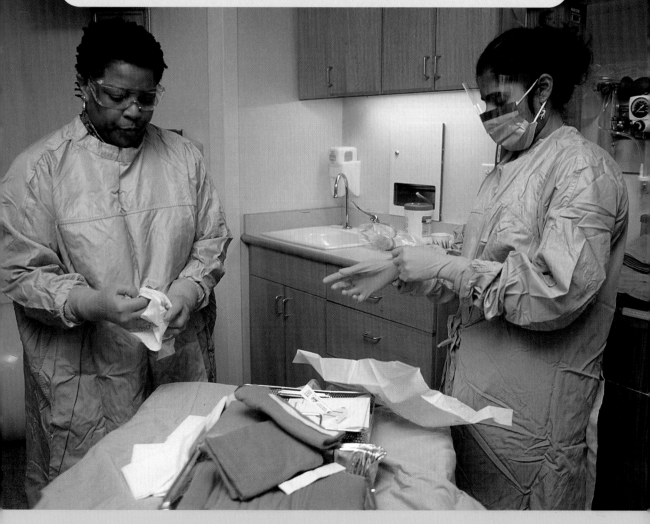

Members of the labor and delivery team get ready for a birth.

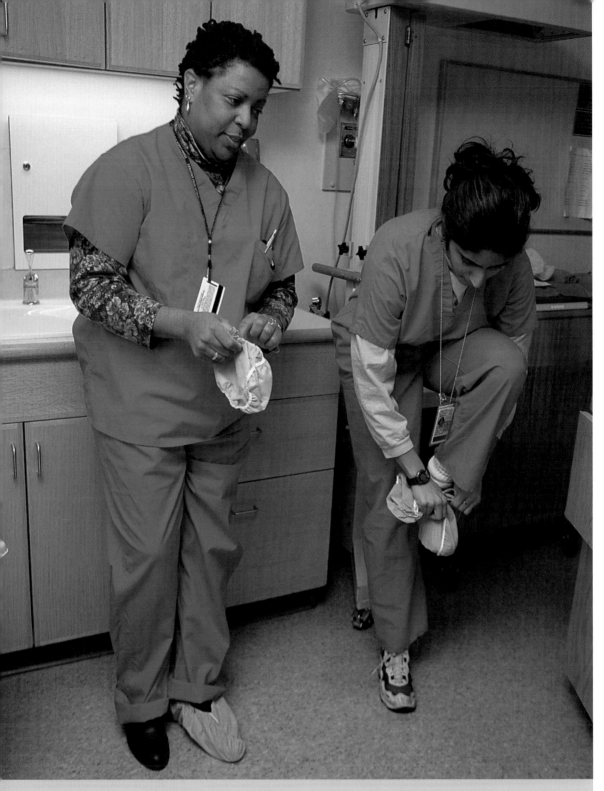

Sterile (germ-free) booties must be worn in the delivery room.

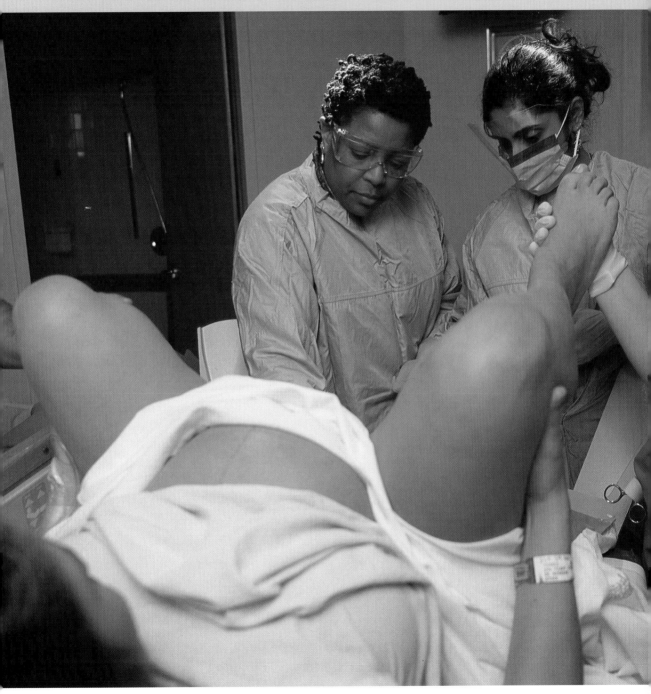

As soon as a baby is born, its mouth and nose are cleaned out with a suction tube. Then it is wiped down and wrapped in blankets.

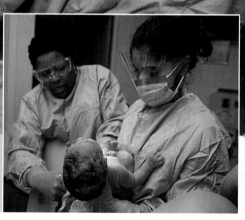

During delivery, the obstetrician, midwives, and nurses make sure that both the mother and baby stay healthy. They help coach the mother through labor, which can be long, painful, and exhausting. When the baby's head comes out, the obstetrician or midwife quickly cleans out its nose and mouth. This is to help it breathe. Then the doctor or midwife helps to deliver the shoulders and the rest of the baby's body.

An important part of an obstetrician's or midwife's job is to care for the baby right after it is born. Within minutes, the umbilical cord is clamped off—this is where the baby is attached to its mother. It is the spot where your belly button is today!

Cutting the umbilical cord, minutes after birth.

Brand new parents enjoy holding their baby for the first time.

The medical team also checks to see if the baby's color is good and makes sure the heartbeat is normal. Then the baby's breathing and muscle activity are checked. The baby is also weighed.

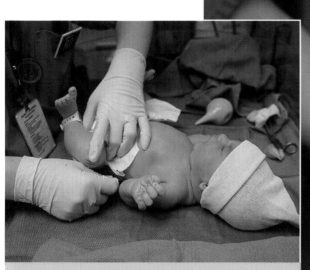

A newborn baby is diapered, dressed, and wrapped in a blanket.

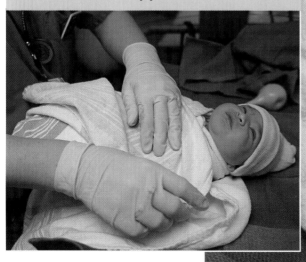

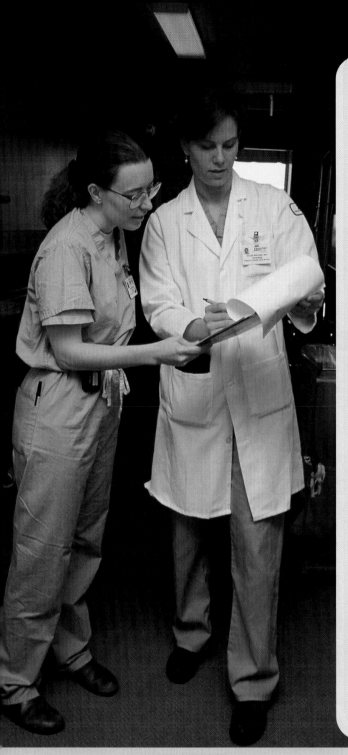

Dr. Wegner checks a patient's chart.

An obstetrician is responsible for any problems during the birth process. Routine deliveries happen when everything goes smoothly and the baby comes through the birth canal and out the vagina. But sometimes such a smooth birth is not possible. This is when the obstetrician may have to remove the baby from the mother with a "c-section" operation. This is one reason why obstetricians are also surgeons.

If your mom or some-one you know has to have a c-section, don't worry—it doesn't hurt and it is very safe. (Mom might just be sore for a few days afterward.)

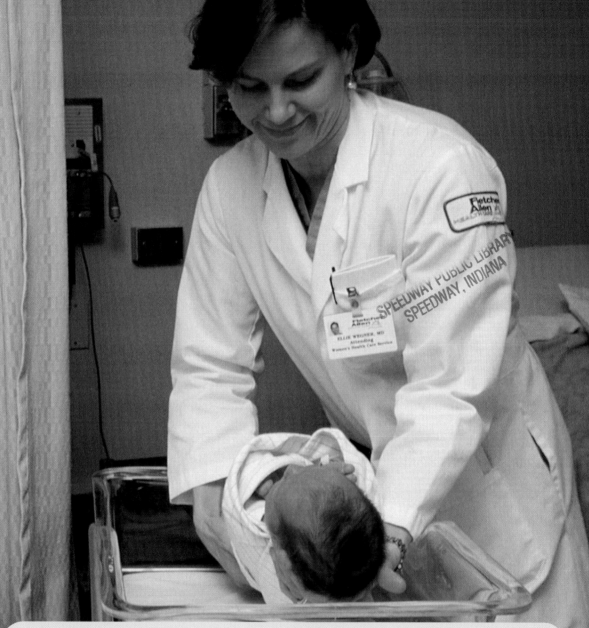

Dr. Wegner leads an exciting and busy life. She is always there for her patients, often for the whole 9 months of their pregnancy. She became an obstetrician because she enjoys being part of the miracle of bringing new life into the world. Each birth produces a unique new person. And that's the magic of what an obstetrician does.

Glossary

embryo (em•bree•yo) The developing fertilized egg during the first 8 weeks.

fertilization The union of a sperm cell and an egg cell.

gestation (jess•tay•shun) The period between the fertilization of an egg and birth.

gynecologist (guy•nek•ol•o•gist) A doctor who specializes in the female reproductive system.

labor The birth process; childbirth.

obstetrician A doctor who specializes in the care of women during pregnancy.

stethoscope (steth•o•skope) An instrument used to listen to sounds made by organs of the body.

umbilical cord (um•bill•i•kal kord) A cord-like structure that connects an unborn baby to its mother's placenta.

vagina Canal and opening through which a baby is passed during birth.

Further Reading

Ganeri, Anita. *Birth and Growth.* Madison, NJ: Raintree Steck-Vaughn, 1994.

Nilsson, Lennart and Lena Katarina Swanberg. *How Was I Born?* New York: Delacorte Press, 1993.

Parramon, Merce. *The Miracle of Life.* New York: Chelsea House, 1994.

Woods, Samuel. *The Pediatrician.* Woodbridge, CT: Blackbirch Press, 1999.

Index